THE ART OF
ARGUMENT

THE ART OF ARGUMENT

Gary Fidel
and
Linda Cantoni

This book was printed in the United States of America.

ThinkLikeALawyer.com, LLC   New York City

Photography credits: Stan Wan and Joyce Coletti

To order additional copies of this book, contact:
Xlibris Corporation
1-888-7-XLIBRIS
www.Xlibris.com
Orders@Xlibris.com

Fidel: To the memory of my father
and with love and gratitude to my mother

Cantoni: To my parents, Matthew A. Cantoni, Jr. (1930-1993)
and Marie L. Cantoni, with love and thanks

CONTENTS

PART TWO: THE COMPLEX ARGUMENT

PART THREE: WRITING THE STORY OF YOUR CLAIM

DISCLAIMER

Although this book is written by lawyers, it is **not intended to give legal advice**. The guidelines and examples we use are intended only to teach a *method* of argument and do not in any way represent advice on dealing with particular legal problems. Your rights and responsibilities in a given situation may vary from state to state, so for help with such problems, consult a lawyer admitted to practice in the state where you live.

INTRODUCTION

The ability to argue—to persuade someone else to see your point of view—is, at bottom, a pretty basic human talent. From about the time we learn to say "Mama" or "Papa," we've begun to argue, in a way—for food, for toys, for just a few more minutes before bedtime. Children are notoriously adept at persuasion; aside from the fact that they're cute and they know it, they have one important advantage over adults: they can't help but be simple and direct about what they want and why they want it.

As we grow up, however, we lose that simplicity and directness. We become complicated, our disputes become complicated, our arguments become complicated. Often when we argue with people, a whole host of facts and emotions crowds our minds, all clamoring for release. We get lost in anger and irrelevancies. We rail against our opponents, and fail to get what we want, because we don't know how to tell them what we want and why they ought to give it to us. We don't know how to organize our thoughts or communicate them effectively. In short, we don't know how to *persuade*.

That's why, in important disputes, people hire lawyers. You might think that what makes a lawyer effective is his or her knowledge of the law. That's only partly true. Most lawyers carry in their heads a good amount of law, but they still have to do some legal research before they open their mouths or put pen to paper. What mainly makes a lawyer effective is that he or she was trained to *think like a lawyer*. Law school teaches would-be lawyers a method of *logical thinking* and *persuasive arguing* that applies to any legal matter or dispute.

Thinking like a lawyer is no deep dark trade secret. Anyone of reasonable intelligence can do it. You don't need three years of law school, $60,000 in student loans, or a three-day bar exam to make a persuasive argument. In this book, we'll show you how to do it and do it well. All it takes is the discipline to organize your thoughts before you express them, and to keep your arguments as simple and direct as possible. We can't guarantee that you'll win every time, but you'll certainly give your opponents a run for their money every time.

PART ONE: THE BASICS

RULE ONE

Argument Is a Craft

Everyone argues. It's a fact of life in our time. We are constantly involved in disputes, major and minor, with everyone from HMOs to the mechanic who services our cars. We all *think* we know how to argue, and that no special knowledge is required to make our point. But nothing could be further from the truth. Argument, whether written or oral, is a craft that must be learned. That principle, more than any other, underlies this book. Everything that follows is designed to teach you that craft. To that end, we teach you to *think like a lawyer*: to use a *method* of argument that, once mastered, will allow you to effectively argue your position in any dispute with anyone over any issue.

The vehicle we'll use for your argument is the **demand letter**. You've probably seen or written these before. It's the letter you write to your insurance company, for example, when it refuses to pay a claim. Or it's the letter you write to your credit card company when it bills you for something you didn't buy. In other words, a demand letter, as we use it here, can be appropriate for just about any dispute. And it isn't just for your opponent; a properly written demand letter is also a good way to present your arguments to a neutral party—a decision-maker—who might have some decisive influence over your opponent's behavior, like the Better Business Bureau or the state attorney general's office.

Throughout this book, we'll show you specific examples of the components of a typical demand letter. And, at the end of the book, we've given you a group of sample demand letters. But you'll soon understand that *all* properly written arguments share a common construction. That's right, *construction*, because the craft of argument is based upon the fundamental principle that arguments are constructed, piece by piece, and effective arguments all share a common structure. Once you learn the craft of argument, you won't *need* sample form letters because you'll be able to *construct* your own.[1]

We've boiled the craft down to 47 essential rules. The contents of this book are organized around these rules, which form the chapter headings. Where appropriate, we illustrate a particular rule with examples taken from the sample demand letters at the end of the book. The first group of 33 rules, in Parts One and Two, applies to constructing the analytical section of your argument: in other words, the *reasons* you should win. The second group of 14 rules, in Part Three, applies to constructing the facts. Although this might seem backwards to you at this point, we've found through experience that it's far easier to master the craft with this approach.

So, let's get started learning how to THINK LIKE A LAWYER!

---

[1]Although we focus on written arguments, all the principles we teach apply to verbal arguments as well.

RULE TWO

The Goal of Argument is To Persuade

The goal of any argument, from your point of view, should be to *persuade* your reader—who may be either your opponent or a decision maker—that you're right. Unfortunately, all too often we throw this principle out the window and instead argue solely for the satisfaction of venting our rage and frustration. To be sure, there's a lot of satisfaction, albeit temporary, in boiling over at the creditor who bills us in error or the insurance company that wrongly rejects our valid claims. But once we simmer down, we're still left with the unsolved problem. Nothing changes, and the rage soon returns, only it increases until it results in actions that we live to regret. The craft of argument replaces venting with rational, goal-oriented action: the goal is *to persuade*, not merely to vent. Persuasion results from proving that your cause is right and just, and that your opponent's action is wrong and unjust. But you can't prove the rightness of your cause if you're shouting or throwing things. All you'll do is frighten or anger the decision maker or your opponent, and that will block any chance you have of winning.

RULE THREE

The Simple Declarative Sentence
Is Your Best Weapon

Let's repeat that: *the simple declarative sentence is your best weapon.*
Remember that grammar class you had in junior high school? The
one you hated? Probably the easiest (and maybe only) principle
you learned in that awful class was that of the simple declarative
sentence: subject, verb, object. Well, to master the craft of argument,
you have only to make use of that one language tool.

A key part of persuasion is making it as easy as possible for the
person you are trying to win over to your point of view to *understand* the basis for your claim. Back when Charles Dickens was
alive, lawyers judged their ability by the number of difficult words
they could string together into tortured and incomprehensible
sentences and paragraphs. Dickens satirized this practice in *David
Copperfield.* In Mr. Micawber's scene of triumph against the slimy
Uriah Heep, Micawber reads a letter accusing Heep of a variety of
frauds, taking particular pride in such legalistic phrases as "To wit,
in manner following, that is to say." The narrator remarks,

> Mr. Micawber had a relish in this formal piling up of
> words, which, however ludicrously displayed in his case,
> was, I must say, not at all peculiar to him . . . In the taking of
> legal oaths, for instance, deponents seem to enjoy them-
> selves mightily when they come to several good words in
> succession, for the expression of one idea; as, that they ut-
> terly detest, abominate, and abjure, or so forth . . . We talk
> about the tyranny of words, but we like to tyrannise over

> them too; we are fond of having a large superfluous estab-
> lishment of words to wait upon us on great occasions; we
> think it looks important, and sounds well . . . [T]he mean-
> ing or necessity of our words is a secondary consideration, if
> there be but a great parade of them.

No longer. Law schools now teach future lawyers to write and speak in clear, easily digestible sentences consisting of simple nouns and active verbs. Legalese, once placed on the throne of legal discourse, is now dead. Simple English is now the mainstay of legal writing and argument. That is because simple declarative sentences are more persuasive than complicated legalese. And that means you don't have to be a lawyer to be persuasive!

Here is the standard definition of a declarative sentence: a sentence that makes a statement. Simple enough. The particular type of declarative sentence that works best in constructing arguments is the *contention*. A contention is simply *the point you're making*. For example: (a) *You block my driveway* every day. (b) When you block my driveway, *I can't get my car out*. (c) As a result, *I'm late for work* every day. As you can see, short, direct statements like these make your position plain. As we work our way through the rules, you'll discover that the craft of argument consists mainly of organizing these short, direct statements—your contentions—in the most logical and effective manner.

RULE FOUR

The More Complicated the Argument,
The Simpler Your Presentation Should Be

This may sound like a paradox, but it isn't. Why? Because the *subject matter* of the argument, whether complicated or simple, is wholly separate and distinct from your *presentation* of the argument itself. Whether you are involved in a long-running and complicated dispute with your HMO, or a much less complicated dispute with a neighbor, the presentation of your argument must be simple and easy to follow. In fact, if you construct your argument properly, the reader will so easily digest it that he or she won't have to read it twice or ask you to repeat it, let alone struggle to understand what you mean. Once you master the craft of argument, you'll be able to "spoon feed" your argument to your reader, no matter how difficult or complex the subject matter.

RULE FIVE

Before You Write Or State Your Argument, You Must Be Sure What It Is

You're probably thinking that this rule is dumb. After all, how can you state or write an argument if you don't know what it is? Exactly. Yet, every day, frustrated people pick up the phone, write a letter, or confront their antagonist personally *without* knowing what they're going to say or write. Oh, they might have a general idea of the point they want to make, but in reality what they *really* want to do is vent. Satisfying your rage will *not* obtain your goal, and will most likely result in your losing credibility or *worse*. During our many years as prosecutors we have seen countless instances where rage provokes rage, resulting in threats and physical violence, even murder. In one case, an otherwise law-abiding family man shot and killed his neighbor because he didn't like where the neighbor put his garbage can and because the neighbor blocked the shooter's driveway with his car at night.

The way to avoid causing yourself even more frustration and misery is to *channel* your anger constructively by taking the time to argue your position in a logical, persuasive manner. Notice we're not saying that you should *set aside* your anger. Far from it. You have good reason to be angry. But the next step, the *only step* that will both satisfy your anger *and* obtain a fair resolution of your dispute, is to construct the most persuasive argument possible. Let your anger motivate you, but don't let it *control* you.

RULE SIX

Stream of Consciousness
Has No Place in Your Argument

Channeling your anger does *not* mean unleashing a wave of vitriol and invective against your antagonist. It means patiently *building* your argument from its most basic, logical pieces, *contentions*. Once those pieces are organized, your argument will come together in a smooth, logical flow that is far more powerful than anger-induced gibberish. Stream of consciousness is as about as effective as driving your car blindfolded. You'll crash mentally without moving one step closer to completing your argument.

RULE SEVEN

An Argument May Be Legal, Factual, Or Both

At the white-hot core of any argument there is a factual or legal dispute. Before we explain that statement, let's define *legal*. We're not *necessarily* talking about laws or regulations or court decisions. While it's possible that one or all of those sources of what lawyers call *black letter law* might be involved in your dispute, it is just as likely that your dispute centers on your *belief* that the unwritten rules of fair dealing, the *common law* that holds our society together, is on your side. Fine with us. At this point, we just want you to understand that when we talk about the *law* part of your argument, we are referring to both black letter law and/or common law. An example of black letter law is a city ordinance that prohibits littering. An example of common law is that it is an unfair nuisance for people to play their stereos at top volume all day and night. Our goal is to show you *how* to use the law to your advantage in your argument.

Now, let's go back to Rule Seven: an argument may be legal, factual, or both. Whatever the specific subject matter of your dispute, it's sure to involve some issue of law, or fact, or both. That means your argument will be constructed of legal contentions, factual contentions, or both. You may have heard the old lawyers' adage: if you don't have the law on your side, argue the facts; if you don't have the facts on your side, argue the law, and if you don't have either the law or the facts, then pound the podium. Our method is designed to teach you how to use the law, or the facts, or both to your best advantage—without pounding the podium.

RULE EIGHT

Contentions Are the Building Blocks of an Argument

Back in **Rule Three** we touched on the major role that contentions—expressed in simple declarative sentences—play in arguments. Let's revisit that now: A contention is *an assertion put forward in an argument*. In other words, it's the point—legal or factual—that you're making. Here's a legal contention: The police can summons you for blocking someone's driveway. (This states the "law"—an ordinance or statute makes it illegal to block someone's driveway, so the police can issue a summons.) Now, look at a factual contention: *You block my driveway every day*. (This simply states a fact.) We've said it earlier, but this is so important we have to repeat it: **The craft of argument consists of organizing contentions in the most effective manner.**

From here on out, everything that follows will build upon the cornerstone of any properly constructed argument, the contention. Sounds simple enough. We all *know* what a contention is. Similarly, we all *know* when someone is arguing effectively as opposed to spouting gibberish. But *knowing* something intellectually and *doing* it well are two very different animals. Practically everyone knows when a movie is good or bad, but only skilled artists are capable of actually *making* a good movie. Merely knowing what contentions are doesn't mean you can automatically know how to use them effectively; you need the skill to use them to construct your argument effectively. All the rules that follow focus on teaching you this skill. Effective arguments, like any other structured creation, are the result of discipline and self-imposed limitations. In order to master the craft of argument, you must become adept at shaping your thoughts according to rigid rules of organization. In formulating arguments, contentions bring order out of chaos: they form disorganized thoughts into weapons of logic.

RULE NINE

A Contention Is a Positive Statement That Can Be Made in One Sentence

There are two absolutes in Rule Nine that you must adhere to: *positive statement* and *one sentence*. While it is possible, of course, to make a positive statement in more than one sentence, even more than one paragraph, for purposes of building an argument you must arbitrarily limit each contention to one sentence. By limiting yourself in this way, you are forced to reduce your anger-induced diatribe down to its most basic elements. Needless to say, in doing so, you'll automatically squeeze flabby chunks of verbiage into tightly compressed declarative sentences that state a positive. So, in writing or speaking your argument, *never* make a contention that can't be expressed in one sentence.

RULE TEN

Your Contentions Must Prove Your Major Claim

Let's start with the new term: **Major Claim**. This is the bedrock claim that you want to make in your argument. It's what you *want satisfied* by your antagonist. For example, if you want your HMO to pay your outstanding bill from a hospital, then you have to make that clear in your Major Claim. In other words, *you want nothing greater* than this from your antagonist.

The Major Claim must state not only your *grievance*, but also the *remedy* that you seek. The whole point of your argument is to get satisfaction in the form of a tangible remedy. It's not enough to simply make it known that you're unhappy about something. That's *not* a claim for purposes of argument. Nor is insulting your opponent or bringing up unrelated grievances. The Major Claim must be as narrow and specific as you can make it. Unlike a contention, the Major Claim can be expressed in more than one sentence. (We'll get to the technique for actually formulating your Major Claim later.)

Now that we've defined Major Claim, we can talk about the relationship between your contentions and your Major Claim. Simply put, your contentions *prove* your Major Claim. That's right: an argument is nothing more or less than a way of *proving* that your Major Claim is valid, through contentions organized in a compelling and persuasive manner. Exactly *how* you go about organizing your contentions will be discussed in the rules that follow.

EXAMPLE

We're now going to introduce our first hypothetical situation. We'll also use this situation as the basis for examples in subsequent rules. At the end of this book are sample demand letters. Our situation concerns **Demand Letters One, Two and Three** and **Trigger Letters One, Two and Three.**

The facts are as follows: Credit Agency sends a collection letter (**Trigger Letter One**) to **Hart Patient** seeking to collect $7,600 on behalf of Anytown Hospital, where Mr. Patient was treated on March 15, 1999. The letter states that the Agency tried to collect from Mr. Patient's HMO, but they declined to pay because the treatment was not covered or the maximum benefit had already been paid. The letter demands that Mr. Patient pay the full amount, and gives Mr. Patient 30 days to dispute the "validity of the debt." Mr. Patient responds with **Demand Letter One**, demanding proof that Credit Agency attempted unsuccessfully to collect from his HMO.

Then, Credit Agency, in **Trigger Letter Two**, again demands payment, attaching a letter that Credit Agency received from Mr. Patient's HMO stating that the $7,600 is not covered by Mr. Patient's insurance. In response, Mr. Patient writes **Demand Letter Two** to his HMO, in which he demands that the HMO pay the full amount and requests that the HMO advise him as to the specific reasons for the denial of benefits.

The HMO responds in **Trigger Letter Three**, giving Mr. Patient the reason for the denial. He then writes **Demand Letter Three**, in which he refutes the reasons for the denial.

As our first specific example, we'll use **Demand Letter One** to illustrate Rule 10.

The Major Claim of Mr. Patient's letter is stated in one paragraph:

"**I dispute the validity of this entire debt, $7,600. My HMO, PAYNOTHING HEALTH CORP., is responsible for paying it.**"

The first part of the Major Claim is Mr. Patient's *grievance*. It affirmatively disputes "the validity of the debt." Note that this is in direct response to the requirement contained in the box at the bottom of **Trigger Letter One** that Mr. Patient dispute the *validity of the debt* within 30 days. By parroting the exact language, Mr. Patient leaves no doubt that he has fulfilled that requirement.

In the second part of the Major Claim, Mr. Patient states his *remedy*. He makes it clear that his HMO is the real debtor, and that Credit Agency should seek payment from that HMO, despite the HMO's assertion that they do not have to pay the bill.

The remainder of **Demand Letter One** is devoted to *proving* Mr. Patient's Major Claim.

RULE ELEVEN

Arrange Your Contentions
In Descending Order of Importance

The architecture of your contentions must follow one basic scheme: arrange them in *descending* order of importance. Why? Because you'll be most likely to grab your opponent's (or the decision-maker's) attention quickly if you start with the most compelling facts and/or the most authoritative rules (the **legal contentions** we mentioned back in **Rules Seven and Eight**) that support your Major Claim.

So, start by deciding on your Major Claim: what do you *really want?* Then, make a list of all the contentions, factual and legal, that you believe will prove your Major Claim. Look it over carefully. What's the most important contention? Put yourself in the shoes of your opponent or decision-maker and determine, objectively, which contention would be the most persuasive, then the second most persuasive, and so on, until you've reordered the entire list.

Now look at the bottom of the list: are there any contentions there that are irrelevant or unnecessary? Don't be afraid to prune them out. When you're making an argument, the more is not necessarily the merrier. Throwing in every fact, no matter how insignificant, will only weaken your argument by boring and/or confusing your opponent or the decision-maker.

The process of listing and sorting your contentions will give you the spine upon which to build your argument. In a sense, you'll be constructing your argument from the inside out.

EXAMPLE

In the second and third paragraphs of **Demand Letter One**, Mr. Patient makes the following **contentions**:

(1) that he is insured by Paynothing (giving details such as his employer's name, how long he's been insured, and relevant identifying information—these are **subcontentions** that prove the main contention that he's insured);

(2) that even Anytown Hospital advised him that Paynothing would cover all the charges;

(3) that he never got a bill from the hospital; and

(4) that Paynothing never sent him a notice disallowing the hospital charge.

Obviously, the most important of these contentions is the first one: that **he is, in fact, insured.** Less important, but still significant, is **what the hospital told him.** Finally, although inconclusive by themselves, are the facts that he **never got a bill** from the hospital and **never got a disallowance notice** from his HMO. These facts tend to support the more important facts circumstantially, making them important enough to include them in the letter, but, because they're not conclusive, not important enough to put right up front.

Notice, too, that Mr. Patient's letter is short and to the point. Everything in it is relevant to his Major Claim. He might have been tempted to insult his opponent, or to write a screed on the nefarious practices of bill collectors. Such "contentions" might have let him blow off steam, but they wouldn't have added anything to the proof of his Major Claim.

RULE TWELVE

A Contention Should Be
The Topic Sentence of Every Paragraph

Remember the "topic sentence" from ninth-grade English composition? A topic sentence is "the sentence within a paragraph that states the main thought, often placed at the beginning." Once you have decided upon your Major Claim and listed all the contentions you'll be relying upon to prove that claim in order of descending importance, you'll have the skeleton of your argument. When you actually start writing out your argument, your contentions will become the topic sentences of your paragraphs. And, to give your argument maximum effectiveness, you must rigidly streamline it: each and every paragraph *must* start with a topic sentence that states a contention. That's right: each and every paragraph should begin with one of your contentions. Your paragraphs will also be organized in descending order of importance, reflecting the relative importance of the contentions that begin them.

EXAMPLE

In **Demand Letter One**, paragraphs 2 and 3 both begin with topic sentences that state a fact contention *proving* the main contention. The most important of the two contentions asserts that Mr. Patient is insured by his HMO. That contention heads up paragraph 2 while the less important contention, that the hospital even advised Mr. Patient that his HMO would cover all the charges, heads up paragraph 3.

RULE THIRTEEN

The Body of Each Paragraph Should Prove The Truth of Its Topic Sentence Contention

Just as each contention must prove the Major Claim, each paragraph must prove the contention that forms its topic sentence. How do you prove a contention? With the facts or law that support your position. Your topic sentence contention will be either fact-based or law-based or both. You'll then back up your topic-sentence contention by *arguing* those particular facts or legal principles that support your contention. Restricting yourself to these guidelines will eliminate any possibility of excess verbiage cluttering up your argument. Your contentions will merge into a seamless, streamlined whole that will give you your best shot at persuading your opponent or the decision-maker that your Major Claim is valid.

EXAMPLE

In **Demand Letter One**, Mr. Patient states in his topic sentence of paragraph 2 that he has been insured by his HMO through his employer since June of 1998. He then *proves* that contention by giving details and providing documentation in the form of his HMO Benefit Card.

RULE FOURTEEN

The Last Sentence of Each Paragraph Should Nail the Proof Into the Reader's Mind

You should never end a paragraph in your argument without a concluding contention. Always keep in mind that the sole purpose of your argument is to persuade the decision maker, or your opponent, that your Major Claim is valid. Argument writing is as different from ordinary communication as solving math problems is from writing a novel. Your argument isn't meant to entertain; it's a weapon you use to win the particular battle you're engaged in. In each paragraph, you make your contention, you prove it, and then you end by telling your opponent or the decision maker *what* you've proven in that paragraph. Leave nothing to chance; use the last sentence of each paragraph to nail down what you've proven in that paragraph.

EXAMPLE

In **Demand Letter One**, the last sentence of paragraph 2 nails down the proof contained in that paragraph by concluding that those facts demonstrate beyond all doubt that Mr. Patient was insured by his HMO at the time he received treatment at the hospital.

RULE FIFTEEN

The Last Sentence of Each Paragraph Should Lead Into the Next Topic Sentence Contention

You know where you're going with your argument, but the reader doesn't. Once you've caught the reader's attention, you want to make your argument unfold so smoothly that it's virtually "spoon-fed." The reader should be able to digest each step in the argument's progression without stopping to think. There should be no confusion. If the reader has to stop and struggle to figure out what you're trying to say, then you've lost ground. The argument should flow uninterrupted to its logical conclusion, and, ideally, the reader shouldn't even be aware that he or she is reading an argument.

The way to maintain the uninterrupted flow of your argument is by using the first sentence of each paragraph as a transition from the previous concluding contention. A paragraph must never simply *begin,* without any tangible relationship to the previous conclusion. Otherwise, the argument will be broken into pieces, losing much of its power.

EXAMPLE

In **Demand Letter One:**

(1) The first paragraph (containing the Major Claim) is connected to the second paragraph (containing the first contention) with the phrase "In that regard," demonstrating that the second paragraph relates to and will prove what's in the first.

(2) The second paragraph is connected to the third (containing additional contentions) by using the transition word, *Indeed*, at the beginning of the topic sentence of paragraph 3. This makes clear to the reader that paragraph 3 will add further support to the fact contentions in paragraph 2.

(3) The third paragraph is connected to the concluding paragraph not with a transition word, but with substance: the third paragraph ends with the contention that the HMO should pay the hospital bill, and the next paragraph tells the reader that Mr. Patient wants proof that the HMO wouldn't pay it.

CAUTION: Transition words are no substitute for actual logical transitions. You can't simply use words like "indeed" to tie completely unrelated contentions together. If you find yourself doing that, then take another look at your contention list: are they in the right order? Are any of them unnecessary? (See **Rule 11**.) Don't "cheat" on this, for you'll only be cheating your argument–and yourself.

PART TWO: THE COMPLEX ARGUMENT

RULE SIXTEEN

The Point Is the Basic
Organizing Tool Of Your Demand Letter

In Part One, we showed you the fundamentals of writing a persuasive argument in the form of a short, simple demand letter. But what if your argument is more complex? For example, suppose you've been going to the same car mechanic for the last couple of years. Your car is fairly new, but every time you bring it in for a routine oil change and checkup, the mechanic finds some major flaw that needs fixing right away and at a lot more than the $30 or so that an oil change costs. After a while, you get suspicious. When he tells you that you need your fan belt replaced—again—to the tune of $500, you tell him you don't have the money to make the repair right now, and you sneak off to another mechanic, who tells you there's nothing wrong. You do some more checking and find out that every other major repair he's made was unnecessary; that some of his former customers had the same experience; and that, even if your car did need the repairs, they wouldn't have cost anywhere near as much as he charged you. You're furious, but you decide not to confront the cheat. Instead, you want to make a consumer complaint to your local attorney general or the Better Business Bureau.

   The situation might require that you present your claim from different angles. In that case, your argument should be subdivided into Sub-Major Claims. You'll still have one, overarching Major Claim; but for the sake of clarity, if you find that you have to advance several unique positions, some of which might be *in the alternative*, then you should further subdivide your argument into additional points, one for each Sub-Major Claim.

Wait just a second, you're probably saying. What's all this about Sub-Major claims and additional points? What is a "point", anyhow, and why haven't we mentioned it before now? Let's pause to define Sub-Major Claim and Point. If your argument goes beyond a simple demand letter, you need to break it down for your reader into sections. Each of those sub-sections should focus on a Sub-Major Claim, a claim that is important enough to deserve its own subheading in your demand letter, but which still fits into the Major Claim. Each Sub-Major Claim will be organized using the Point as the basic organizing tool. We haven't mentioned the Point until now because for learning purposes, you have to understand how to draft a simple demand letter first.

Whether you have one or more points, each point will follow the same basic structure, which we'll discuss below.

EXAMPLE

We're now going to introduce our second hypothetical situation. We'll be using this situation as the basis for examples throughout Part Two. Our situation concerns **Demand Letter Four.**

Here are the facts: Jill Trusting buys a used BMW from Rollback Motors. The odometer reads 38,000 miles and the salesperson, Harvey Slickster, assures her that the car has had only one previous owner, who only drove the car to and from work and treated it like it was a member of his family. Harvey states that to his knowledge, based on the prior owner's representations, the car had no major mechanical problems; nor have the dealer's mechanics, who have thoroughly checked the car, found any significant mechanical problems. The car, he says, is in "tip top" shape. Because it is a reputable dealership, Jill takes Harvey's word and buys the car, which comes with a parts and labor warranty of one year.

Within a month of buying the car, Jill has to take it back to the dealer for major repairs. From then on, throughout the first year, the car is back in the shop every month. After each repair,

Rollback's mechanics assure her that they've fixed the problem. Nevertheless, the same problems recur throughout the year. When the one-year warranty runs out, Jill switches to a new mechanic, a BMW specialist, named Richard Goodlug. He looks it over and tells Jill that the car is in the shape you'd expect given its high mileage. In order to keep the car running, Richard tells her that she should be prepared to spend thousands of dollars in repairs and replacement of major parts over the coming year. When Jill points to the odometer reading, now at 45,000 miles, Richard says that the odometer is wrong, that the car has over 150,000 miles on it, and that those were hard miles, meaning that someone had driven "the hell out of it."

Jill drives to Rollback Motors, where she confronts Harvey with this information. He claims to be shocked and blames everything on the prior owner, who, he says, lied to Rollback when he traded in the car to them.

Jill contacts the prior owner, Mike Leadfoot, who tells her that when he traded in the car to Rollback Motors, the odometer read 175,000 miles, and that he had driven the car "into the ground." The only reason Rollback had agreed to take the car as a trade-in had been that he was upgrading from the 300 series to the 700 series.

Now look at **Demand Letter Four**. We'll examine it in more detail later, but for now, notice how Jill has laid out her complex argument. She starts with an intro paragraph; explains the applicable legal principles; and then weaves together the most important of her facts with the legal provisions to support her claims. She has set out all this in a clear and direct way, using a separate paragraph for each of her two claims, one for a refund and the other for damages. While her argument is more complex than the one Mr. Patient makes in **Demand Letter One**, she uses the same principles to make it just as compelling.

RULE SEVENTEEN

Set Up Your Points

You have to set up your points *before* you actually write them. Whether you use only one point, or multiple points, the actual set up of each point will be the same, structurally. As you've probably figured out by now, a simple demand letter is constructed of one point, while a complex one may have two, three, or more points. But a point is like your audio system—it consists of several different components, which are individually discussed below. But the important thing to remember is that you don't have to use all of these components in every point. You will typically use only those components that are necessary to your individual set of facts and the particular claims that you are making. But to start, we will discuss all the possible components that are available to you when setting up a point.

Here's how to set up each of your points, in a nutshell:

1. Start your point with an **intro paragraph**. In a simple demand letter, this will just be a sentence or two letting the reader know the purpose of your letter, that is, your Major Claim. In a more complex argument, you'll need more, to summarize the Major Claim, any Sub-Major Claims, and a bit of the background. We'll explain this in more detail in **Rule Eighteen**.

2. Next, you'll need what we call a **law paragraph** (or paragraphs). This summarizes the legal principles that apply to your claim. Remember, as we explained in **Rule Seven**, these might be an actual statute, or a clause in a contract, or the "common law" rules of fair dealing, or a combination. (Note: If your argument

relies only on facts, you won't need this component.) **Rules Nineteen through Twenty-Four** will show you how to write your law paragraph effectively.

3. After you've laid out the "law" (if applicable), you can begin to affirmatively prove your claim with **facts**. You'll see in **Rules Twenty-Five and Twenty-Six** the best way to do this.

4. Now you can deal with your **opponent's contentions**, if necessary. **Rules Twenty-Seven through Thirty-One** outline the dos and don'ts of refuting your opponent's arguments and factual allegations.

5. Finally, end your point with a **conclusion paragraph** that sums up your position, as we'll show you in **Rule Thirty-Two**.

EXAMPLE

Demand Letter One does not use all possible point components. It has a minimal introduction and no law paragraph, its second and third paragraphs prove the Major Claim with wholly factual contentions, and its conclusion is also a factual contention.

RULE EIGHTEEN

The Intro Paragraph Sets the Stage

In a demand letter, the intro paragraph is like an announcer who comes out on stage and cues the audience as to the basic situation on stage when the curtain rises. It focuses the reader on the reason for your letter and states the Major Claim.

Often, one or two sentences will accomplish this task. In other instances, it will be necessary to briefly summarize the factual background leading up to your letter before stating your Major Claim.

EXAMPLE

Demand Letter One has a one-sentence intro that states the Major Claim. No factual background is necessary because the letter is in response to Credit Agency's letter, which Mr. Patient encloses.

In **Demand Letter Two**, Hart Patient faces a more complicated situation. He is writing to his HMO for the first time, having already received from Credit Agency a copy of a letter from his HMO to Credit Agency, denying insurance coverage. Consequently, Hart Patient must begin his demand letter with a more extensive intro paragraph in order to provide background information to his HMO that is necessary for his Major Claim to be understood. Once Mr. Patient summarizes the factual background, he states the Major Claim: that he's entitled to full coverage of his treatment at the hospital.

In **Demand Letter Four**, Jill Trusting is confronted by the task of reviewing her year of misery and pulling out the key facts to put into her intro paragraph while she avoids getting bogged down in a too-lengthy background account that will weaken the punch of her intro. Instead of recounting insignificant details, she limits her intro to the landmark facts regarding two issues, the odometer and the repairs on the car:

(1) Odometer facts: the odometer reading when she purchased the car, the odometer reading at the time the prior owner traded the car in to Rollback, and most importantly, that had it not been for the misrepresentation, she wouldn't have bought the car.

(2) Repairs: Despite numerous attempts at repair, the transmission, alternator, drive axle, brakes, steering, and ignition system still malfunction.

She concludes her intro with her demand for a specific remedy—refund of her money in exchange for returning the car to Rollback—which she decides to ask for even though her research of Anystate's consumer fraud statute gives her the right to sue for damages. This remedy is provided for under the Anystate's Used Car Lemon Law.

RULE NINETEEN

Your Legal Principles, If Any, Must Be Stated Before Your Facts

Following your introduction, you have to explain to the reader the legal principles, if any, that apply to your dispute. The legal principles involved will give *meaning* to your facts.

EXAMPLE

Take a look at **Demand Letter Two**. Mr. Patient is claiming that he's entitled to insurance coverage for his emergency treatment. It's all very well for him to say that, but what's his legal authority? The answer is in the policy provision he cites. He tells his opponent (the insurance company) in the *law paragraph* that the policy–essentially a contract between him and the insurance company–covers all emergency treatment in full, without exception. Now his facts–that he's a subscriber and that he got a letter denying coverage–have meaning. Together with the law, they prove Mr. Patient's Major Claim: that he is entitled to full coverage of his emergency treatment.

The law paragraph in **Demand Letter Four** specifically refers to two statutes: Anystate's Consumer Fraud Act and Used Car Lemon Law. Note that Jill tells Rollback the sections of the law she is summarizing (see **Rule Twenty-One**), and she can also attach a copy of the specific statutory language. Those statutes give Jill two possible grounds for getting the result she wants: her money back. Jill states the law objectively (see **Rule Twenty**), in simple English (see **Rule Twenty-Three**), and ends the paragraph with a contention that restates the result she wants (see **Rule Twenty-Four**). She avoids any block quotes from the statutes (see **Rule Twenty-Two**).

RULE TWENTY

Be Objective in Stating Your Legal Basis

Your reader must have confidence that you are fairly and accurately summarizing any applicable legal principles or contract language. To put it another way, if you fail to objectively summarize the legal principles or contractual provisions applicable to your dispute, the reader will no longer have confidence in *anything* that you argue, even if the rest of your argument has merit. Remember, your ultimate goal is to *persuade* your opponent or the decision maker that your argument is logical and fair. Persuasion is impossible without confidence, and once you lose the confidence of your reader, you will have lost the argument. So above all else, when summarizing legal principles, whether statutory, case law, common law, or contract provisions, you must be objective, accurate, and fair.

RULE TWENTY-ONE

Give Clear Citations or Provide Copies of the Law

All the legal authority in the world won't help you unless your reader knows where to find it. He or she will want to look at it for himself or herself to be sure that your reliance on it is valid. So, when you lay out your legal principles, give a *citation* to it. For example, in **Demand Letter Two**, Mr. Patient describes where exactly his opponent can find the authority for his assertion that emergency treatment is covered in full: on page 45 of the policy. He could also, if he wanted, make a photocopy of that page of the policy and enclose it with his letter. If Mr. Patient were relying on a statute, say, a provision of the Insurance Law, he would tell the insurance company what part of the law he's relying on, for example, "Section 323 of the Anystate Insurance Law," and provide a copy for easy reference. This will leave no doubt in the reader's mind as to what the authority actually says and whether it can be relied on.

In short, citations to (or copies of) the applicable legal principles will add credibility, and therefore force, to your argument. Don't forget them.

RULE TWENTY-TWO

Avoid Block Quotes

You might be tempted to quote, line by line, from any *legal* language you believe supports your claim. Whether it's a statute, a case, an administrative decision, or contract language, *don't quote it*. Simply put, block quotes are unreadable. They'll only interrupt the flow of your argument. You should, instead, merely *summarize* the law that you're relying on, in plain English. You can always provide an actual copy of the legal language, as we suggested in **Rule Twenty-One**. As long as you *accurately* summarize the law, there's no need for you to use block quotes. Your argument gains force if it flows, gathering momentum as the logic path becomes clear and irrefutable. When you block flow, you are shutting off persuasive power and breaking up the argument in your reader's mind. Every sentence of your argument should contribute to the argument's flow.

EXAMPLE

In the law paragraph of **Demand Letter Four**, Jill summarizes two different statutes in plain English. If she had used block quotes, she would have stopped the flow of the letter and confused the reader by putting two different statutes, one after another, in the same section. The summary makes clear that the two statutes give her two separate grounds for her Major Claim.

RULE TWENTY-THREE

Translate Legalese Into Simple English

Not only must you avoid block quotes of legal text, you must also avoid turgid quasi-legalese summaries. These stop your reader cold. The reader loses track of your argument, becomes irritated that he or she must struggle to understand what you are saying, and loses confidence in your overall ability to express your thoughts. The fact that you are summarizing legal text won't help you in the reader's eye. Assume that the reader wants your argument spoon-fed to him/her. No matter how intelligent, your reader wants his/her life made easy. The more difficult and complicated the concepts that you are trying to get across, the harder *you* should work to express them in simple, declarative sentences that can be gulped down like ice water on a blistering summer day.

EXAMPLE

In **Demand Letter Four**, Jill summarizes two different statutes without using any legalese. She uses simple, declarative sentences to get to the crux of what these statutes say that's relevant to her claim: Under Anystate's Consumer Fraud Act, General Business Law section 20-99, a consumer who bought something as a result of a material misrepresentation can get damages. And, if the fraud is intentional, the consumer can also get punitive damages. A consumer who buys a used car is also protected by Anystate's Used Car Lemon Law, General Business Law section 120-45. That section requires that a car dealer refund the purchase price, sales tax and fees of a used car when a problem can't be repaired after three or more attempts, or when a car is out of service to repair a problem for a total of fifteen days or more during the warranty period.

RULE TWENTY-FOUR

Conclude Your Law Paragraph With a Contention

You've boiled down any legal language that you're relying on to support your Major Claim. It's as easy to read and understand as the infomercials on the back of a cereal box. You still need a transition sentence that will nail down the law paragraph and set up the next part of your point, the application of the law to your specific facts.

EXAMPLE

In **Demand Letter Two**, Mr. Patient sums up the law by saying, "Therefore, PAYNOTHING must pay in full any claim for any emergency treatment."

In **Demand Letter Four**, Ms. Trusting connects the law to her specific claim by saying, "Either or both of these statutes require Rollback Motors to refund the full purchase price of the lemon you sold me, along with sales tax and fees."

RULE TWENTY-FIVE

Link the Facts to Your Major Claim

The heart of your demand letter is the section that connects your unique facts to your Major Claim. In *your own mind* you can clearly see the linkage between your specific facts and your Major Claim. It's so obvious to you that you see no reason to express it. You assume that your reader is smart enough to make the logical connection by him/herself. Wrong. Don't *assume* anything.

Remember the teacher in grade school who insisted that you *show your work* when you solved a math problem? Back then you probably insisted that just giving the right answer was enough. Your teacher always disagreed, of course. And your teacher was right, because the same is true in argument. You *must show the reader* how you reach your conclusion.

The only way to do this is to patiently work out the logic for him/her through paragraphs that are constructed of contention topic sentences, followed by facts or legal principles that prove your contentions.

How do you link up the facts to each other and then to your Major Claim? Or, if your point is factual/legal, how do you link up the facts and the law to your Major Claim? Well, you *don't* accomplish this by merely restating facts that your reader has already read in your letter. Or, by merely stating the facts for the first time and then stating a bald conclusion. This is the *single most common error* that people make when they add up the facts or when they apply the law to the facts.

In **wholly factual points** (as in **Demand Letter One**), you prove your contentions by showing the reader the overall *factual signifi-cance* of separate relevant facts. You do this by drawing one overarching factual conclusion from relevant separate facts. When considered separately, the facts may lack significance, but when linked together, they prove the truth of your Major Claim.

You'll set up your factual point like this:

Because certain events took place, then, piecing the facts together, only one logical factual conclusion can be reached, the one stated in your Major Claim. Your contention topic sentence states a factual conclusion. Then you prove that conclusion by showing, through inference, *how* your facts add up to that factual conclusion, which supports your Major Claim.

If you're relying on **legal principles** to support your Major Claim, you prove your contentions by showing the decision maker the *legal significance of the particular facts* of your situation. You do this by drawing inferences from those facts. *Because* certain events took place, *then* under the legal principles you have summarized, your conclusion is the only valid one. Your legal principles set yardsticks that are met if certain facts are shown to have occurred. Your contention topic sentence states that the legal yardstick has been satisfied by your specific facts. Then you prove that conclusion by showing, through inference, *how* your facts add up to a factual conclusion that satisfies the legal threshold.

There are no shortcuts. Step by step, contention by contention, you must patiently stitch *relevant* facts to one another or to *relevant* legal principles, until the argument flows together like the seamless images that flash on the screen during a movie.

EXAMPLE

In **Demand Letter Two**, Mr. Patient links his facts (emergency treatment) to the law (policy provision) as follows: *"My treatment on March 15, 1999, was on an emergency basis. Clearly, then, this treatment is covered under the policy provision noted above, and PAYNOTHING must pay for it."*

In **Demand Letter Four,** Ms. Trusting links her facts to the law in two separate paragraphs, the Used Car Lemon Law paragraph and the Consumer Fraud Act paragraph.

In the Used Car Lemon Law linkage paragraph she refers to the service records for her car, which show that repairs were performed on key parts more than three times without success and, in addition, that the car itself was out of service for more than fifteen days for repairs during the warranty period. She links both up with a final sentence: *"Clearly, then, the service history of the car during its warranty period meets the requirements under the Used Car Lemon Law for the full refund I seek."*

In the Consumer Fraud Act linkage paragraph, Ms. Trusting first recites the known facts and then *argues* those facts by drawing the inference that supports her Major Claim: *"Clearly, between the day that Rollback took title to the car and the day that I bought it, the odometer was reset while the car was in Rollback's possession. Because I purchased the car on the basis of the false odometer reading, I am entitled to damages under the Consumer Fraud Act."*

RULE TWENTY-SIX

Legal References Should Be in Plain English

Just as you converted to plain English the legal principles you
relied on in the law paragraph of your point, you must also boil
down to simple English any legal principles that you refer to in
the *linkage* paragraph of your point. In other words, don't repeat
the legal principles verbatim or try to make them more flowery
this time around—you'll only bore the reader. Either summarize
them simply, or refer the reader to the law paragraph in such a way
that it's clear what you're relying on.

EXAMPLE

In **Demand Letter Two,** Mr. Patient applies the law to the facts in
a simple manner by stating that his treatment was on an emergency basis and referring the reader to the preceding law paragraph: *"Clearly, then, this treatment is covered under **the policy provision noted above,** and PAYNOTHING must pay for it."* Mr. Patient
could also have briefly summarized the legal principle this way:
*"**Because the policy provides that all emergency treatment is covered in full, without exception,** PAYNOTHING must pay for my
emergency treatment."* Either way is effective, so long as the reader
can understand what exactly you're referring to.

In **Demand Letter Four,** Ms. Trusting applies the Used Car
Lemon Law to the facts in one sentence: *"Those records prove that
all of the parts that I mentioned above were repaired three or more
times by your service department during the year the car was under
warranty and that the car was out of service for more than fifteen*

days to repair some of these problems during the warranty period."
The black letter law is integrated *into* her factual contention, leading to the conclusion that she has met the act's requirements for
relief. Similarly, in the next paragraph she applies the Consumer
Fraud Act to her facts in two sentences: *"Clearly, between the day
that Rollback took title to the car and the day that I bought it, the
odometer was reset while the car was in Rollback's possession. Because I purchased the car on the basis of the false odometer reading,
I am entitled to damages under the Consumer Fraud Act."* The
black letter law is not repeated—it is enough for her to assert that
she purchased the car as a result of a material representation, i.e., a
false odometer reading.

RULE TWENTY-SEVEN

Avoid the Straw Man

A common error in making an argument is to attack your opponent's contentions *before* you've affirmatively proved your Major Claim. It might seem attractive to set up a straw man only to knock him down. But it's not very effective. All it does is call too much attention to your opponent's position, and not enough to yours.

If you've followed the format we've laid out for you so far, you've already avoided the straw man because your point now has an intro paragraph, a law paragraph, if applicable, and a linkage paragraph where you have stitched together relevant facts, or the applicable law, if any, to your specific facts. In short, you've completed the *affirmative* section of your point. Now you can, if appropriate, address your antagonist's claims.

In most demand letters you won't have to do this. In **Demand Letters One and Two**, for example, the affirmative contentions refute the creditor's demand for payment, and there's no need to address it in a separate paragraph or section. In **Demand Letter Three**, which is more complicated, Mr. Patient must address PAYNOTHING's contention that he should have called the hotline. He does so after making his affirmative argument that he believed that the hospital was going to notify PAYNOTHING. **Demand Letter Four** presents a different situation because it states a claim and gets the ball rolling. The target of the letter, Rollback Motors, would either agree to the demand or fire back a response letter denying any and all liability. The high stakes for the dealer—

admitting fraud—would probably result in a stalemate that would lead to litigation. (Note: Even if you don't need this section in your demand letter, the following rules will help you prepare for oral argument, which will most likely take the form of a telephone call with your adversary.)

RULE TWENTY-EIGHT

Don't Address Every One of Your Opponent's Contentions

There will be situations where you make your affirmative argument and still feel that you should separately attack your opponent's contentions. Or, you may be involved in a telephone argument and your adversary may confront you with specific contentions. How do you deal with them?

Your opponent, like yourself, will have one or more points, but only one Major Claim. Don't make the mistake of answering each and every claim or contention made by your opponent. Your argument will bog down in endless *back and forth*, and all you will do is bore your reader or, worse, make your opponent's contentions appear valid by overemphasizing them. Now that you understand the basic structure of any well-constructed argument, you can figure out where to best aim your attack. Select those contentions, either legal or factual, that are the linchpins of your opponent's argument. If you can knock those out, the rest will collapse of their own weight.

RULE TWENTY-NINE

Attacking Your Opponent's Legal Principles

First, look at your antagonist's legal principles. Chances are that he or she has misread or ignored contract language, a court decision or a statute, or cites law that does not apply to your situation. Or, he or she has misstated the applicable law. Or, he or she has ignored legal principles altogether, relying instead on a general sense of outrage and allegations of unfairness.

The best way to attack faulty legal principles is to correct them. By going beyond mere assertions that your opponent's version of the applicable law is wrong, and asserting once more the correct legal principles, you not only destroy the legal foundation for your opponent's conclusions, you also reinforce in the reader's mind *your* summary of the law.

Even if your opponent's legal contentions are correct, you can still point out that he has misapplied them to the facts of your case. This leads us to the facts and the inferences to be drawn from those facts.

RULE THIRTY

Attack Your Opponent's Facts

You must also review your opponent's version of the facts, and the inferences that he or she draws from those facts. One or both prongs may be vulnerable. Your first line of attack will be the accuracy of your opponent's version of facts. Obviously, there may be a total disagreement between you as to the facts at issue in the dispute. Those are known as issues of *credibility*. In other words, who's telling the truth? If you're involved in a dispute before an arbitrator or hearing officer or judge, he or she will resolve those factual disputes by deciding whose version is credible. We'll show you how to write your own persuasive factual summary below.

Your second line of attack is more subtle. Even if your opponent accurately recites the facts underlying the dispute, he or she may draw completely different inferences from those facts. You must attack your opponent's inferences, showing how they are simply unsupported by the uncontested facts.

For example, in **Demand Letter Three**, Mr. Patient is refuting PAYNOTHING's contention that he should have called its Healthline before receiving treatment (see **Trigger Letter Three**). In our sample letter, he recounts that when he presented his insurance card to the hospital cashier, she told him that the hospital would notify PAYNOTHING of the treatment and that PAYNOTHING would pay for it, adding that Mr. Patient has nothing to worry about because the hospital deals with them all the time. Suppose, however, she says only, "We deal with them all the time." Mr. Patient would have to *infer* from her statement that

PAYNOTHING would be notified and would pay his claim. PAYNOTHING might not dispute the fact that the cashier made the statement. Instead, it could argue that it wasn't reasonable for Mr. Patient to *infer* from the statement that PAYNOTHING would be notified and would cover his claim. It could argue that, at best, the cashier was just remarking that she'd dealt with PAYNOTHING in the past, and that Mr. Patient wasn't entitled to infer anything else from her statement. To support his inference, then, Mr. Patient would have to rely on additional facts: he didn't get a bill from the hospital, and PAYNOTHING didn't notify him that the hospital was seeking payment from them.

RULE THIRTY-ONE

Avoid the Defensive

Attack your opponent's account of the law, attack his facts, distinguish, turn to your advantage, or dispute, but *do not apologize.* Whether you're writing a demand letter or making an oral argument, you must not allow yourself to be put on the defensive. Does that mean you should lose your temper, shout or become irrational? Of course not. To some degree, you're always defending your position. The crucial distinction is one of *tone.* Even if you're on the defensive, you must avoid *sounding* like you're on the defensive. Your written points should have a tone that is as immediate as the actual sound of your voice. You must always take a positive tone, emphasizing the affirmative, even when you are defending your position.

This is especially true in oral argument. In oral argument you must keep the structure of your written argument in mind. Your written contentions will enable you to defend your position in a positive manner by providing you with the points you want to make. If you're under attack during an oral argument (most will be on the phone), fall back on the proof that you've developed to support the contention under attack. You may find yourself repeating the same contentions over and over again, but that's unavoidable, particularly when the attacker continues to hit you with the same objections. Always maintain your poise and your positive tone. By positive we mean confident, without sounding arrogant or condescending. Always be firm, but respectful of your opponent and of the decision maker.

RULE THIRTY-TWO

End Your Point With a Conclusion Paragraph

Once you've finished attacking your opponent's contentions, you must return to the affirmative by concluding your point with a paragraph that mirrors your intro. This paragraph, like the intro, will once again restate your Major or Sub-Major Claim. You should resummarize the major contentions that support your Major or Sub-Major Claim. Your final sentence should be your Major or Sub-Major Claim, stated as an absolute conclusion supported by all that has come before it. If you have an alternative demand of your own (for example, pay or explain), you can add it here.

EXAMPLE

In **Demand Letters One and Two**, Mr. Patient's conclusion paragraphs not only restate his Major Claim, they also make counterdemands (in the first, proof that the insurance company refused to pay the claim; in the second, an explanation). In **Demand Letter Three**, Mr. Patient restates his Major Claim in the course of listing the consequences of PAYNOTHING's failure to pay for his treatment, and by adding that he will take legal action against them if they don't pay.

RULE THIRTY-THREE

An Argument Is a Unified Entity

We've broken points down into components: intro, law, linkage section, attack section, conclusion. But each of your points should flow together, a unified set piece whose components merge together into a coherent seamless whole. The components will merge only if you bind your contentions and subcontentions with neon-sign topic sentences and paragraph-ending sentences that set up the topic sentences of the next contention paragraph.

All of the principles we've shown you in this section are the same principles lawyers use when they make their arguments. This is what they get paid for and why the good ones win cases. It's what **thinking like a lawyer** is all about: channeling your anger in an organized way that effectively presents your claim and maximizes your chances of winning.

Now that you've mastered the art of argument, we'll show you in the next section how to think like a lawyer when it comes to presenting your facts. You could have all the legal right on your side, but you could still lose if you don't coherently tell your story.

PART THREE: WRITING THE STORY OF YOUR CLAIM

RULE ONE

Tell a Story

You probably associate *story* with a lie. This stems from childhood, when stories are told to us or when as children, we made up events and were chided for telling stories. But the ability to write a compelling *story* is crucial in argument craft. Your opponent or the decision maker will want to know the factual basis for your claim, and you must be able to convey those facts in a way that emotionally involves the reader and prepares him/her for contentions that you'll use to construct your argument.

EXAMPLE

Both **Demand Letter Three** and **Demand Letter Four** tell a story when they recount the facts. **Demand Letter Three** recounts that Mr. Patient suffered sharp pains and became dizzy while driving, that he drove to the nearest emergency room because he thought he was having a heart attack, that he was immediately taken to a treatment room where he received a three-hour battery of tests. He then learns that he suffered an anxiety attack, which triggered his chronic asthma. The story continues as he recounts his release from the hospital and the payment arrangements that justified his decision not to notify his HMO. This story has a beginning (the alleged heart attack), a middle (the treatment) and an end (his release from the hospital). It is not a description of events. It is a *recounting of them.*

Similarly, in **Demand Letter Four,** Ms. Trusting tells the story of how she bought the car, how it developed severe mechanical problems, and how she came to realize that the odometer reading on the car was false. Even though she tells this story in less than a paragraph, it also has a beginning (her purchase), a middle (the mechanical problems) and an end (her discovery that the odometer reading was false). She could have written a more detailed and extensive version of the story, but the short one serves just as well in this particular case because her letter is designed to state her claim and it is in her interest to get to the argument section as quickly as possible.

THE ART OF ARGUMENT

RULE TWO

Be Accurate and Objective

Your opponent or the decision-maker will be persuaded by your recitation of the facts underlying your claim only if he or she believes that you've recounted them in an accurate and objective manner. *Any* misrepresentation of the facts, no matter how slight, will inevitably destroy your argument. The more objective you are in your account, the more reliable your version of events will be.

RULE THREE

Don't Argue or Characterize the Facts

One of the oldest clichés is that there are two sides to every story. You can't escape this fundamental aspect of life. Your opponent is convinced that certain events took place, while you view those events from a completely different point of view. Because you know how your opponent sees things, you'll be tempted to argue over certain disputed facts or characterize specific events. Don't. You'll only weaken your narrative by interrupting its flow, and highlight your opponent's account of disputed incidents.

EXAMPLE

Both Mr. Patient and Ms. Trusting avoid characterizing specific events. Thus, Ms. Trusting never alleges that she was "cheated" or that Rollback's employees "lied" to her. The facts speak for themselves, more powerfully than any characterization of them.

RULE FOUR

Make a Chronology

An *event* is an occurrence. Someone has to do something for an event to occur. Dig out the events that make up the history of your dispute. List those events in chronological order. Now you have the spine of your narrative of events. In most cases you should recount those events in your letter in that same chronological order so it's coherent. But in some cases, as in **Demand Letter Four**, you should recount the events in a different order so as to emphasize certain of the events.

EXAMPLE

The *event spine* for **Demand Letter Four** consists of the following, in chronological order:

1. Ms. Trusting purchases the car;
2. The odometer reading at time of purchase is 38,000 miles;
3. During the first year, the car suffers endless mechanical problems;
4. Once the car is out of warranty, Ms. Trusting learns from the prior owner that the odometer read 175,000 miles at the time Rollback took it as a trade-in.

In her account, Ms. Trusting changes the order, choosing to emphasize two facts: that when she purchased the car, the odometer read 38,000, and that she had recently learned that when traded in, the car's odometer read 175,000 miles.

RULE FIVE

Banish the Passive Voice

The next step is to make those events come alive on paper. To do so, you must use the active voice. Excise any passive verbs and replace them with active verbs to depict each event of your narrative spine.

Let's look at two ways to tell a story, one in the passive voice, one in the active voice:

PASSIVE: The witch was pushed into the oven by Hansel and Gretel. She was baked into a giant gingerbread cake by the fire. Then she was eaten by the children.

ACTIVE: Hansel and Gretel pushed the witch into the oven. The fire baked her into a giant gingerbread cake. Then the children ate her.

Notice how the active voice is more compelling—and easier to read. It invites the reader to visualize what happened as if it were happening right now. By contrast, the passive voice slows the reader down. He or she has to wait until the end of the sentence to figure out who was doing what. The last thing you want to do is delay the reader when you're presenting your facts. Keep it clear and crisp by keeping your account as active and immediate as possible.

Sometimes, of course, the passive voice is appropriate. For example, in **Demand Letter Three**, Mr. Patient says, "I was immediately taken to a treatment room." He uses the passive voice here because either he doesn't know who exactly took him there, or it's not important who took him there. (He could have said, "An orderly took me to a treatment room," but that's not particularly important.) But you should use the passive voice seldom. Read through your facts after you've written them and see whether you've used the passive voice anywhere. Then start editing. Try to turn every passive phrase into an active one, where you can. You'll wind up with a much more effective statement of facts.

RULE SIX

Rely on Bare Facts

Let the bare facts convey your underlying message. Don't adorn the basic elements of your story with commentary or opinion. You'll only weaken the effectiveness of your narrative. Opinion or commentary break the flow of your narrative, making the reader aware that you're trying to manipulate him/her. Your narrative should have the clarity of spring water flowing over a rockbed. The reader should never become conscious of your guiding hand. Rather, he or she should be swept along by the momentum of the facts as your version of events moves to its conclusion.

EXAMPLE

Both **Demand Letter Three and Demand Letter Four** recount the facts in an objective but compelling manner. In both letters the clarity of the narrative makes the facts compelling without elaboration or hyperbole.

RULE SEVEN

Close the Gaps

Your narrative should be complete, but not overly detailed. Depict an event in concise sentences, leaving out irrelevant minor details. Concentrate on the behavior at the core of the event. All else is excess verbiage. Relate the spine of events, one at a time, describing behavior and conversations.

Don't leave out any relevant events, even if they hurt your position. Any substantial gap in your narrative will sidetrack your reader and cause him/her to wonder why you've left something out. He or she will no longer trust your rendition of the story, and you'll lose some, if not all, credibility. Once you have the spine of events down on paper, link them up with transition phrases.

EXAMPLE

Compare the concise narrative of the facts in **Demand Letter Four** to the account of the entire story (see the **Rule Sixteen** example in Part Two). The story contains many more events than Ms. Trusting chose to include in her spine of events. But she decided that she would gain more power by recounting only the most important events, as opposed to the details of what the salesperson said to her at the time she purchased the car and what the second mechanic said to her regarding the car's advanced mileage.

RULE EIGHT

Don't Run From Inconsistencies

You can't avoid inconsistencies. Your argument will be destroyed if you fail to acknowledge inconsistencies or facts that hurt your case. Your opponent will hammer you with those very facts and the decision maker will reject your version of events. Every case, no matter how strong, has its weaknesses and flaws. You must embrace them. By doing so, you'll deaden their sting. Your goal must be to make the decision maker trust your narrative of events as complete, reliable, and objective.

EXAMPLE

In **Demand Letter Three**, Mr. Patient recounts how he went to the emergency room because he felt like he was having a heart attack. He also mentions, however, that an examination revealed that he did not have a heart attack and that he was released. Now, of course it would have helped his argument to show that he was seriously ill, but he can't lie about that. Nor can he simply ignore it. He has to face these facts head on, or he will lose credibility. He does so and quickly moves on to show why he believed he was covered: the cashier's statements leading him to believe that the hospital would notify the insurance company, and the lack of a bill or claim rejection.

RULE NINE

Separate Real World Events From Dispute Events

Long-running disputes tend to engulf the participants in a torrent of documents and appearances before decision makers. As the dispute encompasses more and more time, it becomes more and more difficult to recount the core events that sparked the dispute. Your factual narrative must focus on the real world events that incited the dispute in the first place, not the tortured history of the dispute once it became the subject of a paper war. The account of the core events may be much shorter than the history of the dispute if you've been going back and forth with your opponent for a long time.

What *should* you do with dispute events? The dispute history should be recounted—if it's relevant—*after* your real world events. At some point in time, one side or the other may file a claim or a complaint with a decision making body. You may have done so by sending a letter to an institution or organization, or by using appeal procedures put in place by the corporation with whom you have a dispute. The filing of a claim or taking of an appeal always comes after the real world events that are at the core of the dispute. In your narrative of events, use subheadings to separate the sections depicting real world events from dispute events.

EXAMPLE

There are several stages in poor Mr. Patient's quest for coverage of his medical claim. First, he gets **Trigger Letter One** from the collection agency, demanding payment for his hospital treatment.

He responds with **Demand Letter One**, declining to pay unless he gets proof that his insurance company refused to cover the claim. This prompts the collection agency to provide the proof with **Trigger Letter Two**: the insurance company's letter stating that Mr. Patient's policy doesn't cover the treatment he got. Mr. Patient then sends **Demand Letter Two** to the insurance company, demanding that it either pay his claim or explain why it won't do so. The insurance company comes back with **Trigger Letter Three**, in which it explains that Mr. Patient didn't follow its rules by calling its Healthline.

These letters lay out the dispute, but they're *not the real-world events at the heart of the dispute*. The real-world events are in Mr. Patient's **Demand Letter Three**, in which he *tells his story*: that he felt like he was having a heart attack, that he went to the emergency room for treatment, and that the cashier told him that the hospital would notify the insurance company and that the insurance company would pay the claim. These are the facts that directly support his Major Claim. His previous correspondence with the collection agency and the insurance company is *not even mentioned* in **Demand Letter Three**, because it doesn't do anything to prove his Major Claim.

If, however, Mr. Patient were taking his claim to a higher authority—the Better Business Bureau, say, or his state's insurance commissioner—he'll want to recount ALL the events, including the correspondence, to show how the dispute started and why he's still dissatisfied. In that case, he'll tell the story of the correspondence AFTER he's told the story of his illness and treatment.

RULE TEN

Put Subheadings in Their Place

Subheadings are useful organizers, but don't become addicted to them. They should never be used in place of transition or introductory sentences. Even if you use them, your narrative of the facts should flow as if the subheadings weren't there. Like chapter breaks in a novel, your subheadings should reorient the reader's focus without disturbing the overall flow of the narrative. Keep them to a minimum, and use them only when your narrative is particularly complex. For example, you might use them when relating a lot of different events that occurred at different places at the same time.

RULE ELEVEN

Dialogue Adds Realism

The events that make up the spine of your narrative will inevitably involve conversation between the participants. You can make those events come to life with quotations, but make sure that the quotes are relevant to the issues in dispute. There is no point in quoting speech just for the sake of adding dialogue. If relevant, speech is as much a form of action or behavior as physical action.

EXAMPLE

In **Demand Letter Three**, Mr. Patient tells of his conversation with the hospital cashier partly by paraphrasing what she told him and partly by quoting. The quotes he uses emphasize the paraphrases. "Nothing to worry about" and "we deal with them all the time" bring immediacy and interest to the story, and show why Mr. Patient believed her when she told him that the hospital would notify Paynothing and that Paynothing would cover his claim. He doesn't need to quote her at length or word for word; in fact, that would slow down the story.

RULE TWELVE

If You Have a Source, Cite It

Just as you should cite to the sources of the legal principles you're relying on (see **Rule Seven**), you should also cite to documents such as letters or contracts when you refer to their contents in your factual narrative. If you're narrating real world events that don't have a written source, you won't be able to give a cite. Nevertheless, you should be careful to be as accurate as possible in your account of such events—especially conversations—because those events may *become* the subject of a judicial proceeding. If that happens, you could be legally bound by the version of events that you recounted in your demand letter.

RULE THIRTEEN

Complex Facts Require Simple Narratives

In his novel, *Bleak House*, Dickens tells the story of a lawsuit that
has continued, unresolved, for so many decades that it has taken
on a life of its own, and only highly paid lawyers can figure it out.
We hope your dispute won't imitate art. But your dispute may
involve multiple real world events stretching over a period of weeks
or months or even years. No matter how complicated a history
your dispute has, you must narrate that history in a simple, direct
manner. The basic chronological narrative structure applies to both
single-and multiple-event narratives.

EXAMPLE

Compare **Demand Letter One** with **Demand Letter Four**. The first
has a very simple set of facts, the second a more complex set of
facts. Yet **Demand Letter Four** is just as clear in its account of the
facts as **Demand Letter One**, because the story is told simply, directly, and in a logical order that emphasizes the most important
facts.

RULE FOURTEEN

Your Narrative Should Be Riveting But Reliable

To the outside world the subject matter of your dispute may seem unimportant. But not to you. If you weren't emotionally committed to your claim, you'd have no interest in arguing it. Your narrative should reflect your emotional involvement. The purpose of narrative structure is to channel your emotion in a constructive direction, to give it focus. When you depict the event or events that make up your dispute, convert your anger into words by making your account riveting. If you don't care, no one else will. On the other hand, if you engage in unfocused histrionics, your version of events will be rejected as the product of an unstable personality. Again, the point of structuring your narrative of the history of the dispute is to focus and channel your anger by making the facts come alive for the decision maker.

Adopt a tone that is objective. Channel your anger into flow and structure, but keep it out of the language you use. The facts themselves, if organized in a riveting narrative, will show the reader that you have a valid factual basis for your arguments. The reader must reach this conclusion on his/her own. If you browbeat the reader, it will only make him/her distrust your narrative. If you are objective in your presentation of the facts, the reader will trust your narrative. But trust can only come from within. You cannot impose it from without.

EXAMPLE

In **Demand Letter Four**, Ms. Trusting's taut account of the facts
and straightforward demand for a refund convey her anger and
determination to prevail far better than a verbose, openly angry
letter. Similarly, in **Demand Letter Three**, Mr. Patient's account of
his attack conveys the fear and panic that he experienced in a manner that lets the HMO know that he won't back down.

CONCLUSION

Think Like a Lawyer

Now you've unlocked the secrets of the craft of argument: Organization, clarity, and logic. It's how lawyers can win their cases, and it's how you can win them, too. Does this mean you can go out and represent yourself in a complex lawsuit? No. The old saw that the man who represents himself has a fool for a lawyer and a jackass for a client is still true. If you must go to court to resolve your dispute, get a lawyer. But if you're trying to *avoid* a lawsuit, you'll make your best pre-emptive strike if you think like a lawyer.

APPENDIX:

Sample Letters

TRIGGER LETTER ONE

WEASEL CREDIT AGENCY
2000 Mean Street
Anytown, Anystate 11111

January 1, 2000

Hart Patient
1500 Leafy Road
Anytown, Anystate 00000

Re: Client: Anytown Hospital
Patient: Hart Patient
Treatment Date(s) 03/15/99
File Number RA456-000923
AMOUNT DUE: $7,600.00

Dear Hart Patient:
The account listed above has been referred to us for collection. We have first attempted to collect the amount due from your insurance carrier/health maintenance organization; however your carrier has informed us that either a) coverage is not available, or b) you have paid maximum benefits to which you are entitled.

Accordingly, you are responsible for paying the remaining amount due in full.

Please send your payment to us and enclose the form on the back of this letter.

ONE OF OUR ACCOUNT REPRESENTATIVES IS AVAILABLE TO ASSIST YOU.

Very Truly Yours,
Weasel Credit Agency, Inc.

UNLESS YOU DISPUTE THE VALIDITY OF THIS DEBT, OR ANY PORTION THEREOF, WITHIN THIRTY DAYS AFTER RECEIPT OF THIS NOTICE, WE WILL ASSUME THAT THE DEBT IS VALID. IF YOU NOTIFY US IN WRITING WITHIN THE 30 DAY PERIOD THAT THE DEBT, OR ANY POR-TION THEREOF, IS DISPUTED, WE WILL MAIL YOU VERI-FICATION OF THE DEBT OR A COPY OF A JUDGEMENT. FURTHER, UPON WRITTEN REQUEST WITHIN 30 DAYS AFTER RECEIPT OF THIS NOTICE WE WILL PROVIDE YOU WITH THE NAME AND ADDRESS OF THE ORIGI-NAL CREDITOR, IF DIFFERENT FROM THE CURRENT CREDITOR.

DEMAND LETTER ONE

January 10, 2000

Weasel Credit Agency
2000 Mean Street
Anytown, Anystate 11111

Re: File No. RA456-000923

Dear Sir or Madam:

With respect to the enclosed "debt notice," please be advised that I dispute the validity of this entire debt, $7,600. My HMO, PAYNOTHING Health Maintenance Corp., is responsible for paying the entire amount.

In that regard, I have been a patient/subscriber of PAYNOTHING since my employer, Anytown Hardware, contracted with that HMO in June of 1998. My certificate number is 88888888, my group number is 444F757 and my category is 321D. Attached is a photocopy of my PAYNOTHING Benefits Card. There can be no doubt, therefore, that I was, at the time of my treatment at Anytown Hospital from 3/15/99 to 04/1/99, a subscriber of PAYNOTHING HEALTH CORP.

Indeed, upon leaving Anytown Hospital, I was advised that the entire bill for my treatment would be covered by PAYNOTHING. Anytown Hospital has sent me no bill or explanation for the $7,600 charge you claim I owe. Nor have I ever received notice from PAYNOTHING that there was any such charge, or that PAYNOTHING disallowed any such charge. Consequently, PAYNOTHING is fully responsible for paying the $7,600 you claim is due.

Until I receive satisfactory proof that you attempted unsuccessfully to collect this from PAYNOTHING, I must dispute and decline to pay this charge.

Very Truly Yours,

Hart Patient
1500 Leafy Road
Anytown, Anystate 11111
999-888-7777

Enc.

TRIGGER LETTER TWO

WEASEL CREDIT AGENCY
2000 Mean Street
Anytown, Anystate 11111

January 16, 2000

Hart Patient
1500 Leafy Road
Anytown, Anystate 00000

Re: Client: Anytown Hospital
Patient: Hart Patient
Treatment Date(s) 03/15/99
File Number RA456-000923
AMOUNT DUE: $7,600.00

Dear Hart Patient:
In response to your letter of January 10, 2000, we are providing verification of the above listed debt.

Accordingly, you are responsible for paying the remaining amount due in full.

Please send your payment to us and enclose the form on the back of this letter.

ONE OF OUR ACCOUNT REPRESENTATIVES IS AVAILABLE TO ASSIST YOU.

Very Truly Yours,
Weasel Credit Agency, Inc.

encl.

TRIGGER LETTER TWO ATTACHMENT

PAYNOTHING HEALTH MAINTENANCE CORPO-
RATION
P.O. Box 8540
Anytown, Anystate 11111

October 12, 1999

Weasel Credit Agency
2000 Mean Street
Anytown, Anystate 11111

Re: File No. RA456-000923

Dear Sir or Madam:
In response to your inquiry, our records show that the amount in question, $7,600, is not covered by the named subscriber's policy.

Accordingly, we are not responsible for payment of this amount in whole or in part.

Very Truly Yours,

John P. Rogers
Vice President

DEMAND LETTER TWO

February 2, 2000

John P. Rogers
Vice President
PAYNOTHING Health Maintenance Corp.
P. O. Box 8540
Anytown, Anystate 11111

Re: File No. RA456-000923

Dear Mr. Rogers:

I am writing this letter to advise you of an erroneous denial of insurance benefits by PAYNOTHING HEALTH CORP. I have been a patient subscriber of PAYNOTHING since my employer, Anytown Hardware, contracted with PAYNOTHING in June 1998. My certificate number is 88888888, my group number is 444F757, and my category is 321D. Attached is a copy of my PAYNOTHING benefits card. Under my policy, I am entitled to full coverage for my treatment at Anytown Hospital on March 15, 1999.

My policy with PAYNOTHING states, on page 45, that all emergency treatment is covered in full. No exceptions are listed. Therefore, PAYNOTHING must pay in full any claim for any emergency treatment.

My treatment on March 15, 1999, was on an emergency basis. Clearly, then, this treatment is covered under the policy provision noted above, and PAYNOTHING must pay for it.

Nevertheless, on January 21, 2000, I received for the first time a copy of a letter that you sent to Credit Agency dated October 12, 1999 (a copy is attached). You advised Credit Agency that PAYNOTHING declined to pay, in whole or in part, the $7,600 owed Anytown Hospital for my treatment. You further advised Credit Agency that the charges were for treatment not covered by my policy with PAYNOTHING. You did not notify me that you would decline coverage, and you have no explanation of why the treatment was not covered.

In view of the clear policy provision covering all emergency treatment without exception, you cannot refuse to pay this claim.

I therefore demand that you pay this claim forthwith as per the policy provision, or explain your refusal to do so in detail.

Very Truly Yours,

Hart Patient
1500 Leafy Road
Anytown, Anystate 11111
999-888-7777

Enc.

TRIGGER LETTER THREE

PAYNOTHING HEALTH MAINTENANCE CORPO-
RATION
P.O. Box 8540
Anytown, Anystate 11111

March 8, 2000

Hart Patient
1500 Leafy Road
Anytown, Anystate 00000

Re: File No. RA456-000923

Dear Subscriber:

Your claim has been reviewed and denied.

You failed to comply with the following policy requirements: (a) You must call our hotline as soon as possible
before any urgent admission; (b) You must call our hotline
within 24 hours of any emergency admission.

Both of these requirements are printed on the back of
your insurance card. Printed in bright red on the front of
your insurance card is the following advisory: **You must call
Paynothing Healthline before hospitalization or surgery.
See back of card for details.**

Thank you for your inquiry.

Very Truly Yours,
John P. Rogers
Vice President

DEMAND LETTER THREE

March 12, 2000

John P. Rogers
Vice President
PAYNOTHING HEALTH MAINTENANCE CORP.
P. O. Box 8540
Anytown, Anystate 11111

Re: File No. RA456-000923

Dear Mr. Rogers:

I am in receipt of your letter of March 8, 2000.

I dispute your denial of my claim. I demand that PAYNOTHING cover the entire amount of $7,600. With this letter I appeal your denial of my claim to your claims review panel.

The facts regarding my treatment are as follows: On March 15, 1999, I was driving to work when I felt sharp pains in my chest, became dizzy, and experienced shortness of breath. Thinking that I was having a heart attack, I drove to the nearest emergency room, which was Anytown Hospital. Although I walked into the ER, I was gasping for breath and the pain in my chest felt like a steel vise. I told the admitting person that I was having a heart attack and I was immediately taken to a treatment room.

Three hours later, after numerous tests, Doctor Stone advised me that I had not had a heart attack. The tests failed to show any sign of cardiac arrest or arterial blockage. Doctor Stone concluded I had suffered an anxiety attack, which in turn had triggered my chronic asthma.

At the time of my release from the ER, I went to a cashier. At that time I and presented my PAYNOTHING insurance card. The cashier told me that the hospital would notify my insurance company of my treatment and that "I had nothing to worry about," as PAYNOTHING would cover the entire bill. "We deal with them all the time," the cashier related. Believing that the hospital would notify you, I saw no need to call the PAYNOTHING HEALTHLINE.

My belief was reasonable and justified under the circumstances. This was, after all, a situation where the insured must notify the Healthline *after* treatment. This was not a situation where PAYNOTHING could have refused to authorize treatment or required a second opinion. Whether I notified you or the hospital notified you, the result would have been the same: the charges were already fixed, the treatment concluded.

Not only was it reasonable for me to conclude that the hospital would notify you, nothing occurred following my release to make me think otherwise. I never received a bill from the hospital. Nor did PAYNOTHING ever notify me that it had received a request for coverage from the hospital and had denied that request. I was thus justified in concluding that you had been notified by the hospital and that my insurance covered the bill in full.

Because of your wrongful refusal to cover this charge, a collection agency is now threatening me with legal action. This will damage my credit rating, and I may have to incur legal expenses defending myself against legal action to collect the debt. If PAYNOTHING continues to refuse to cover the amount due, I will take legal action against you.

Very Truly Yours,

Hart Patient
1500 Leafy Road
Anytown, Anystate 11111
999-888-7777

Enc.

DEMAND LETTER FOUR

February 1, 2000

Mr. Omar Pricelow
President
Rollback Motors
25 Rip Off Highway
Anytown, Anystate 11111

Dear Mr. Pricelow:
On December 28, 1998, I purchased a 1989 BMW 325e
from your dealership. At the time I purchased the car, its
odometer read 38,000 miles. I have recently learned that
the odometer reading was patently false, and that at the
time the car was traded in to Rollback Motors by its prior
owner, the odometer read 175,000 miles. Had it not been
for Rollback's misrepresentation of the mileage on the car, I
would not have purchased it. In addition, despite repeated
attempts at repair during my warranty year, the transmission, alternator, drive axle, brakes, steering, and ignition system still malfunction. That being the case, I demand that
you refund the purchase price in full, and sales tax and fees,
and I will gladly return the car to Rollback Motors.

Under Anystate's Consumer Fraud Act, General Business Law section 20-99, a consumer who has made a purchase as a result of a material misrepresentation may recover
damages. Moreover, if the fraud is intentional, the consumer
may also recover punitive damages. A consumer who buys a
used car is also protected by Anystate's Used Car Lemon
Law, General Business Law section 120-45. That section
requires that a car dealer refund the purchase price, sales tax,
and fees of a used car when a problem cannot be repaired
after three or more attempts, or when a car is out of service to
repair a problem for a total of fifteen days or more during

the warranty period. Either or both of these statutes require Rollback Motors to refund the full purchase price of the lemon you sold me, along with sales tax and fees.

As your own service records show, I am entitled to return the car to you for a full refund under the Used Car Lemon Law. Those records prove that each of the parts that I mentioned above was repaired three or more times by your service department during the year the car was under warranty, and that the car was out of service for more than fifteen days to repair some of these problems during the warranty period. Clearly, then, the service history of the car during its warranty period meets the requirements under the Used Car Lemon Law for the full refund I seek.

Although I am entitled to a full refund solely on the basis of the Used Car Lemon Law, there is yet another ground for my claim under the Consumer Fraud Act. On the date that you sold me the car, the odometer reading of 38,000 miles was incorrect. Although you certified in writing when I bought the car that at the time you received the car from the prior owner it had an odometer reading of 37,750 miles, the prior owner, Michael Leadfoot, told me that the odometer read 175,000 miles on the day that Rollback took title to it. Mr. Leadfoot's statement is supported by a copy of the odometer certification that he gave to you when you took title. That certification has 175,000 miles entered in the box for the car's odometer reading on that date. Clearly, between the day that Rollback took title to the car and the day that I bought it, the odometer was reset while the car was in Rollback's possession. Because I purchased the car on the basis of the false odometer reading, I am entitled to damages under the Consumer Fraud Act.

At this point I am demanding only that Rollback refund the full purchase price along with sales tax and fees. I will keep this offer open for 10 days. If you fail to respond in that period, I will turn the matter over to my attorney with instructions to litigate this matter to the full extent allowed by law.

Sincerely,
Jill Trusting

WARNING: The "law" cited here is fictional. It is solely meant to illustrate the manner in which a law paragraph should be written. It is not a legal citation or recommendation of a particular legal theory to be pursued by the reader. Readers should consult with an attorney before pursuing a specific legal claim. There are many different legal theories of liability and non-lawyers may forfeit valuable legal rights by pursuing a claim without seeking advice from a trained professional.